Big Emotions, Stepping Stones
© 2020 by Pam Bowers and Kim Bowers

Written by Pam and Kim Bowers
Illustrated by Nadia Ronquillo

All rights reserved. No part of this publication may be reproduced, stored in retrieval system, or transmitted in any form by any means — electronic, mechanical, photocopy, or recording in any form — except for brief quotations in printed reviews without prior permission from the authors.

This is a work of fiction. Names, characters, places and incidents are products of the authors' imaginations or are used fictitiously and are not to be construed as real. Any resemblance to actual events, locales, organizations or persons living or dead, is entirely coincidental. While all attempts have been made to verify the information provided in this publication, neither the author nor the publisher assumes any responsibility for errors, omissions, or contrary interpretations of the subject matter herein. Interpretation and application are the sole responsibility of the purchaser or reader. The advice and strategies found within may not be suitable for every situation. This work is sold with the understanding that neither the author or the publisher are held responsible for the results accrued from the advice in this book. You should consult with a health professional for further details and further actions.

Published in La Vergne, Tennessee by Ingramspark

Cataloging-in-Publication Data has been applied for and may be obtained from the Library of Congress.

ISBN 978-0-578-73670-9

Printed in USA

Mfr: DSC / LaVergne, TN USA / August 2020

Table of Contents

- **8** Sadness
  - 8 Missing Parents
  - 10 No Friends to Play With
  - 11 Unkind Words

- **12** Anger
  - 12 Someone Took Something
  - 14 Getting Corrected
  - 16 Follow the Rules
  - 18 Correcting Others

- **20** Moodiness
  - 20 Tired/Crabby
  - 22 "Hangry"
  - 24 Asked to Do Something

- **26** Shyness
  - 26 Meeting New Adults
  - 28 Meeting New Kids

- **30** Worry
  - 30 Grandpa is Sick
  - 32 Sibling Is Hurt

- **34** Fearfulness
  - 34 Flying on an Airplane
  - 36 Monster in the Closet
  - 38 Scary Bugs & Things

How to Read this Book

Parents, Families, and Caregivers,
We designed this book to be a tool to help you topically address and maneuver through current daily struggles in your child's life. Different from many of its counterparts, this book does not have a narrative story, but rather is meant to be a platform for conversation between you and your child. It can be used both retrospectively and proactively to help your child prepare for and learn how to handle their big emotions. Additionally, because of the non-narrative style, you can skip around the book in any order as your child needs...you don't need to read it cover to cover! Pick a scenario as the need arises and discuss them one at a time.

The pictures are the driving force of your conversation—feel free to examine every inch of them! Every two pages focus on a single scenario. We suggest you start with the image on the left as it initiates the scenario whereby the character is struggling to work through their big emotions. Then, examine the page on the right. This side revisits the scenario introduced on the left, but shows the character successfully navigating their big emotions. Each image also comes with a series of questions on a sticky note, which serve as a starting guide to help you and your child talk about what you see in each image, the difference in the characters' reactions, and how your child reacts similarly or differently. As you both get comfortable with this inviting learning and sharing style, you will find it easy to eventually think of your own questions to emphasize other characteristics you'd like to work on.

Start with the guiding questions to begin conversations around emotions and responses, and then move to the practical section (the big paragraph on the right page) to enhance your discussion. Each practical section includes various combinations of validation (e.g., "There will be many times in life that you will feel sad--and that's okay"), normalization (e.g., "When we feel this way..."), coping strategies (e.g., "...take a break from the game or your group of friends and take a couple breaths"), and guiding principles (e.g., "Let your fears help you make smart choices, but don't let them keep you from doing things you'll be proud of doing later.") to help you as caregivers open the lines of communication with your child and set them up for success. These practical sections can also serve as models for you to create your own discussions. Revisiting these scenarios often can help your child grasp these concepts and apply them as life happens.

The general structure of the book and practical sections come from our collective experiences as a mother, an educator, a coach, and a graduate student. We have found that using this structure and these strategies have been helpful for the children we interact with. As fellow friends, caregivers, and educators, we hope aspects of our models will be helpful for you and yours. Although what we give to you in this book comes from our own personal experiences, we have come to know that scholarly research shares many commonalities. References are available on our website at www.smoothsailingbooks.com.

We wish you all the best in your journey! Remember, growth is not always easy, but it is often worth it in the end.

Your Friends,
Pam & Kim

There will be many times that you feel sad—and that's okay! We can't always control the things in our life, but we have choices we can make when we feel. Talking to others we trust about our feelings can be a great way to help us work through how we're feeling. People like our grandparents, parents, teachers, and friends are good people to talk to. They are special people that have been put in our lives so that they can help us understand why we are feeling sad and how to work through our sad feelings so that we can be joyful again.

Calm Down Tip: *If you're feeling too sad to talk about how you feel, you can first stop to find all of the blue things around you. By taking a minute to notice these things, we will calm our minds and bodies enough to talk about our sadness.*

Sometimes finding friends to play with can be hard. Your friends might want to play something different or they might want to play with other people. Either way, it can make you feel sad, mad or both! It's okay for our friends to make those choices. Even though our hearts hurt, we need to allow our friends to be friends with others—and they need to do the same for us. This is what good friendship is all about! When we start thinking this way, it will help us understand our feelings, then we can continue to do fun things like finding new friends to play with.

Two is *better* than one!

When people say unkind things, it can really hurt our feelings. We might want to cry, be embarrassed, or be mean back. We may even want to change how we look or what we like to fit in. If we let what others say tell us who we should be, then we will never be ourselves. It matters more what you believe about yourself, than what others think of you. You are special! All your likes and dislikes, favorites and least favorites make you, you! You can still be kind to others while still being yourself. When this happens, think of all the things that you like about yourself.

Anger

"Hey, that's mine!"

"Give it back!"

"I'd be mad, too, if someone took my yarn ball."

Discussion Questions

For this page

1. What do you think is happening in the picture?
2. How is Amani feeling?
3. What might she be thinking? What about her face and body show you this?
4. What is Amani doing because of her feelings?
5. How do your face and body look when you feel this way?
6. What do you do when you feel this way?

For that page

7. Revisit questions 1-6 with the other image.
8. What is different about Amani's reaction here than in the other picture?

Sharing is not always easy, especially if we need to share something we really love. We might think that the other person might break it or ruin it, but if it's something your parents would be okay with you sharing, then you should share it! Everything we have is really a gift, so if we really think about it our parents, families and friends are actually sharing with us! Isn't it cool that others share with you? Knowing that others are sharing with us will help our hearts want to do the same for others, because we know how fun it is to be shared with!

Sometimes it doesn't feel good to be told that what we're doing is wrong, but what we need to remember is that the truth is helpful. Hearing the truth helps us grow and learn. Whether we are in karate class, at school, or at home, we need to make sure that we are listening and obeying. It is important to follow the rules and to respect the people in charge. When we listen to the truth, it helps our minds and bodies grow—and even keeps us and others safe!

When others do something wrong, it can make us feel angry. We have the choice to be mad about what others are doing or we can try to understand why they did what they did. When you feel this way, take a break from the game or your group of friends and take a couple breaths. You'll often regret saying unkind things out of feeling hurt, but you'll never feel bad about calming down before speaking—two wrongs don't make a right! Taking a minute to calm down allows us to help others make better choices, so that everyone can play together kindly.

Calm Down Tip: During your break you can look for all of the red things around you and take deep breaths. Then, once you have calmed down enough you can go back to your friends and work through what is making you upset.

Moodiness

"But, I don't want to take a nap!"

"A little cat nap wouldn't hurt..."

Discussion Questions

For this page
1. What do you think is happening in the picture?
2. How is Amani feeling?
3. What might she be thinking? What about her face and body show you this?
4. What is Amani doing because of her feelings?
5. How do your face and body look when you feel this way?
6. What do you do when you feel this way?

For that page
7. Revisit questions 1-6 with the other image.
8. What is different about Amani's reaction here than in the other picture?

Sometimes we don't know what is best for us, especially when what is best is not what we want to do. Our bodies can make us feel cranky when we are tired. We might not want to do things or we might cry. This is our body's way of asking us to rest. When we feel this way, playing with our friends, watching TV, or playing a videogame may seem way more fun, but it's not going to give our body the rest that it needs. Taking care of ourselves is important! Because when we are well rested, we can actually enjoy our favorite things more!

Okay, I'm a little tired.

Can I watch my show when I wake up?

Woo Hoo!

Naptime!

Waiting is not easy, especially when you are waiting on food. Your tummy might hurt, you might feel a little shaky, or you might feel annoyed; this is your body's way of reminding you to have something to eat. When we feel this way, we need to try our best to be patient while we wait for our food. Even though our bodies are struggling, we don't have the excuse to be unkind. Asking for a small snack using our kindest words is a good way to help our tummies calm down and help us be kinder while we wait.

Calm Down Tip: To help you wait patiently for your food, find something to play with or to do to keep yourself from thinking too much about how much you want that PB&J—or even better— help make your own snack with someone old enough to help you!

When we are doing something we love, it can be hard to put it away and listen to our parents. Obeying, while it might not be what we want to do, will end up making our hearts happy because the directions come from people we love. Often, we are asked to do things because it is what is best for us. When we trust that our parents only ask us to do what is good for us, then it makes obeying easier.

Meeting new people is not always fun or our favorite thing. We can feel nervous, worried, or embarrassed. It is important to recognize that we feel these things when we meet new people, because it is very possible that the person we are meeting feels the same things, too! Instead of thinking only about how we're feeling, if we think about how the other person is feeling and we try to make them feel more comfortable, everyone will walk away feeling happier.

Meeting new kids may not always be our favorite thing to do. We like our old friends or we like our family better. At the same time, we need to be willing to meet new friends because our old friends might not always be there. Sometimes they move, sometimes we move, or sometimes we're just not at the same place, but change can be fun! You never know what cool people you'll get to meet! How you think about meeting new people can change the way you feel about it. If you think about the fun you'll have with the new people, then it makes meeting them easier.

Not knowing exactly what will happen or how it will happen can make us feel worried, especially when it comes to the people we love. When we become worried, we ask a lot of "What if" questions that we don't have answers to and that might make us feel worse! The good news is that we can change the way we think about what is worrying us. So, instead of asking the "What if" questions, start thinking of things that you know are true. When we think this way, it will help calm our hearts and give us courage.

I don't know when Grandpa will be all better, but I do know that they will give Grandpa good doctors.

When we get worried, our minds may think that bad things are going to happen. Just because we think these things, doesn't mean that we have to believe them! A broken arm might really just be bruised; a forever-lost toy might just be under the couch. To keep ourselves from believing these ideas, we can pause and ask ourselves if we know these things are happening or if we just think they are. Doing this helps keep us from believing things that aren't true and allows us to remain in control of our thoughts.

"I want to say that her arm was broken—that was a big fall!"

"But, I don't know that for sure. Maybe it's just bruised."

Flying on airplanes, riding on trains, going on roller coasters, singing on stage—there are a lot of things that can make us fearful. We cannot fly the plane, control the weather, or decide how other people will respond to us, but we can control what we do with those feelings. Being afraid can be good because it can help us be aware of what is going on around us; at the same time, being afraid can also keep us from doing fun and awesome things. Let your fears help you make smart choices, but don't let them keep you from doing things you'll be proud of doing later.

Calm Down Tip: Take deep breaths in through your nose and out through your mouth, pretend you're blowing bubbles or blowing out a candle!

Periodic Table

Shadows and the dark can be very scary. We cannot see what is in front of us, so our minds can trick us into thinking things are there that actually are not. It is always okay and good to ask for help, but know that you are brave and strong too! Made-up monsters can only make us scared when we focus on how scary they are instead of how brave, strong, and powerful we are.

Okay, Sparkles.

Here's the plan: I know that I can do hard things and that mom is just down the hall.

I'll go check the closet myself and will call her if I need her.

Calm Down Tip: If you're feeling scared, worried, insecure, anxious, etc. saying things that affirm who you are, what you are capable of doing, and that you are loved can be a great tool to help you work trough your feelings.

"AHH!!"

"There's a huge spider!"

"It looks big enough to eat me!"

Discussion Questions

For this page
1. What do you think is happening in the picture?
2. How is Noah feeling?
3. What might he be thinking? What about his face and body show you this?
4. What is Noah doing because of his feelings?
5. How do your face and body look when you feel this way?
6. What do you do when you feel this way?

For that page
7. Revisit questions 1-6 with the other image.
8. What is different about Noah's reaction here than in the other picture?

Big bugs and creepy crawlies are really cool to some kids, but to many they are very scary. If you see one, you may be afraid that it will hurt you. While we still need to be careful around these creatures, we don't need to be scared. We can use self-control, which means to stop and think before we act, to help us in these situations. Using self-control, we do not hit a bee if it lands on us, kick away a snake that's in our path, or chase away a big bird. Instead, we slowly walk away and tell an adult. Doing this keeps both us and others safe.

Big Emotions, Stepping Stones
© 2020 by Pam Bowers and Kim Bowers

Written by Pam and Kim Bowers
Illustrated by Nadia Ronquillo

About the Authors:

Pam and Kim Bowers are a mother-daughter writing team. Pam is a World Top 50 Master Junior Golf Instructor with a passion for child character development. Kim holds a B.A. in Psychology and an M.Ed. in Curriculum & Instruction, Elementary Education. She is currently working on her doctoral studies in School Psychology.

Together they share a rich history in growing through many of life's seasons as a mother and daughter with a best-friendship forged by tears and laughter. Their years of experience, adventures, and God-given talents lend a unique and practical perspective in creating tools to help support children and their parents/care-givers.

About the Illustrator:

Nadia Ronquillo is a children's book illustrator, visual development artist and content creator from Ecuador. After receiving her Bachelor's in Graphic Design and Audiovisual Production, she started freelancing as a children's book illustrator and collaborating remotely as a visual development artist with studios in Latin America. She is now developing a tv series show for kids.

For more, visit www.nadiaronquilloart.com and @nadiaronquilloart on Instagram.

Hide and Seek

Find me

Hey! My name is **Swish**. I belong to Noah. I love swimming in my bowl and watching Noah play video games.

Hi, I'm **Pudge**. I live with Amani and her family. My favorite thing to do is take naps. I love Amani and Jada, even if they put me in crazy outfits sometimes.

Hey, I'm **Tut**!

A simple turtle, living his best life! Lily and her family take good care of me. I love watching Lily do her experiments — she has the craziest ideas!

Hi! My name is **Chirp**! I'm a bird who loves to travel, hang out in trees, and watch my favorite kids learn and grow.

Hello, I'm **Pepper**. Liam and his family are my favorite people. I love helping Liam and his siblings bake — especially when they drop icing onto the floor.

www.ingramcontent.com/pod-product-compliance
Lightning Source LLC
Chambersburg PA
CBHW042029090426
42811CB00016B/1792